Gallery Books
Editor: Peter Fallon

THE BALLYCONNELL COLOURS

Dermot Healy

THE BALLYCONNELL COLOURS

Gallery Books

The Ballyconnell Colours
is first published
simultaneously in paperback
and in a clothbound edition
on 30 October 1992.

The Gallery Press
Loughcrew
Oldcastle
County Meath
Ireland

ISBN 1 85235 102 0 (*paperback*)
1 85235 103 9 (*clothbound*)

The Gallery Press receives financial assistance from An Chomhairle
Ealaíon / The Arts Council, Ireland.

Contents

Although I know the road
I will never reach Córdoba.
— Lorca

The Two Lakes

'Conn flows into Cullen, and Cullen into Conn.'
— James Joyce, *Finnegans Wake*

1

One star
Becomes two
In a trough of waves
That splash
Like trout.

2

The moon
Falls as snow
On speckled fields
Of rock.

3

Lough Conn
Is birdless.
So where

Does the singing
Come from?

PART ONE

LOUGH OUGHTER

1970-1975

The Moths

Into my room come moths,
butterflies and insects
blown from the hill;

they inspect themselves
in the glass, tuck wings
and sleep gracefully.

If a light goes on
in the middle of the night
the great waltz begins.

The womb that bore them
had room for little things —
flight-ashed wings that

throw huge shadows, till
at dawn this host
will brave the wind.

Nightfishing

Leaving the pub early
we cut a long arc
of silence through Kinale,
the waves running up our arms.

Flat water closed over the moon
and the hollow moon
sank below the clouds. Far off
we reel in long memories,

the deep shadows of fish.
Voices of distant fishermen
come-and-go with the up-and-down
of the bottomless water.

The echoes drum below us.
From down there the darkness
surfaces, and swims across the sky.
At the end of your oar is a splashing star.

A car pushes its headlights
through two hills. It swings
a sudden light round the lake.
My father has aged.

We are crudely aware of each other's
face. Pike shiver in the wet keel.
Oarlocks shunt. We travel over
sleeping cities

till at last we enter the acres of reeds.
They close in before us and behind.
They tick against the prow
like kitchen clocks.

Now whatever we've done
and whatever we'll do
matters not. Forever we are
rowing with one rustling oar

on water, through the dark,
towards home. The day catches
the pale reflection of our boat;
then the reeds close in again.

Forever we are out there
with the hour hand of the reeds
on the prow and the second hand
of the reeds on the keel.

Washed by rushes
we dip through the shifting mist.
The boat makes the least sound.
The panic in my heart

beats louder in yours
till eventually my life without you
opens up before me.
Near Brian McHugh's we meet land

at last. We tie up to a tree
as the fog lifts. Then relax
from the hold of the water
turning under our feet,

the oars turning under our arms.

Party Line

When I stopped praying
so many nightmares ago
I gave up solemn occasions.

But in my own way
I joined hands
and celebrated with wine

the phrases I got in a
lucky-bag from a priest
twelve Christmases ago:

arc of the covenant,
gate of heaven,

morning star.

Recovery

in memory of Charlie McGovern

1

The first thing I hear is women's voices,
the next a priest withdrawing from me.
A friend leaves by the bedside
Berryman's *Seven Addresses to the Lord*
which I must have asked for

and then you
climb in the window

(funny to fall asleep at last
in the ladies' ward and outside
the drunken gardener falling
asleep under
the purple plum).

2

Night nurses water the flowers;
St Joseph guards my window,
a giant shadow thrown across the room at night in prayer.
And after being moved from the women's ward
they find room for me in the men's.
Charlie, after a lifetime of coughing,
lies across from me.

You can make any tree weep, he explains,
if you train it. A man in the corridor drops dead
after weighing himself on the scales.
Did the second hand register his soul leaving,

flying off? And a woman is saying:
It will be easy to satisfy me now,
I wouldn't dream of spending
half the night up now,
oh God, no.

3

When your head begins to swing to the right
we'll correct the tendency,
when your head begins to swing to the left
just shout for me, the doctor said,

and then the veins begin to gather
like gnarled roots
at the back of my head.

4

You're one of the lucky ones, says the doctor,
Usually they die.
The one sure thing is
it can never happen to you again.
That's something, I suppose,
I say.

5

In a local news item in the *Anglo-Celt*
a man is described who died
after receiving a prick
from a rose in his garden,

the following week
his brother was shot by gangsters
in New York.

So what do you make of news like that?
I feel like Virginia Woolf
when she stood under the vast dome of the British Museum

and felt as if she were a single thought
in that huge broad forehead.

6

How many thoughts can one cram into a day?
How many of us are in this world
rising up and doing a little,
going some of the way,
being there at the time,
in the early morning meeting them
down the side streets,
the sound of shoes, steps being washed down,
coal dropped into a hole in the street?

An example of sublime scepticism
is the man who discovered purgatory.

Charlie McGovern,
after a lifetime in the air force
where he saw coffins come back from Vietnam
filled with dope,
left his apartment in the States,
just turned the key in the lock,
and came home to die in Ireland.

And then today
Charlie McGovern
saw an X-ray of his lung
which he prayed was not his,
one big white mushroom

rising over Glengevlin.

7

Poor Charlie,
highest nut in the wood,
man of the limestone-white neck,
now you are heartbroken and fallen on hard times,

a herb of grace is needed for your wound
or young women who in the heat-haze of noon
might pluck for you *moonógs*
from down at the black rocks;

not for show you constantly shrug your shoulders
and stay awake most of the night,
your last horse stands in the gorse haggard
looking at the same spot for days,

your dogs have strayed from you
to the Maguires and the O'Rourkes
and sometimes you stop at the gate
watching for them, whistling,

and Pilib, when winter freshened his wound,
departed beyond the wounded Boyne,
he sends neither message nor friends to bring good news
but the heart has only what it is accustomed to,

so you follow with affection tales of his,
news of great victories,
thousands of foreigners dead,
while in your innermost heart

you found the shaft
enter his heart,
and his memory in your mind
will long be a reproach to you —

Pilib breathless in death
propped up in his coffin
like in the prow of a currach.
Afterwards you cross through Dowra

like a man astray in the head
and try luring birds from the cliffs
that you might have some sign of the future,
acknowledgement from the blackfaced queen

that she might send you easy peace terms.
But the news is not good.
The last time I saw you you were trying to sit up in the Home.
They were shooting the hereafter into your veins.

8

In the miraculous country of silk
where the horse runs with one foot
poised on the wings of a swallow

and the natives refrain from saying
the names of women who are called by the names of flowers
or the names of men who are called by the names of birds

lest they awake a sleeping ancestor,
so, Charlie, I say your name low.
As I recovered you were dying,

the priest suddenly came out from behind the screen,
and across sand and muffled stones
the undercurrent bore your soul away.

9

In Killygowen
all rested and well
I feel another
heart beating by my side,
joy all round.

The first day I go to town,
an off-duty soldier speaking of grief
congratulated me
with a flick of his fingers.
'I saw you at the funeral,'

he says.
I look at him a long time
trying to gauge who has died.
'It was good of you,' he says, 'to come.'
'It was nothing,' I replied.

Your Beautiful Coat

Purple trumpets
Blow in the weeds.

Green-winged butterflies feed off
The purples and mauves of May.

Insects sail
Over the beeches and pines.

On the island April shelters
Among the yellow and frosted green.

I am lucky that you are here
To see all this.

This red thrilling insect
Would make a beautiful coat, you say,

This jet of colour
Is all I could desire,

And look, the reeds
Are high as

The baby's chin.

Animals

I knock the cat
absentmindedly off
my lap. She sits facing
the empty far wall

making me feel rejected.

❧ ☙

On Monday
I tied up the dog
because the spring
lambs were being born,

and threw his smile away.

❧ ☙

On Harold's Cross Road
we ran into
a scruffy stray mongrel
with no tail,

which recognised both of us immediately.

❧ ☙

When the cat died
of cat flu, the kitten
looked round anxiously
at night,

waiting for the sneeze in the dark.

Photographs 1970

1. In the Dismal Evening

In the dismal evening,
in the long night

when pages are short,
nothing forgives the mind

so much as
a tree

talking to itself in leaf language
in a park quiet as the dark palm of your hand,

and the ages, like dark horses,
trotting the length of your window sill;

after and beyond our small lives
the deep rain coming down the side of the sky.

2. *Today*

Today
I have watched them
as the earth moved round the sun
and the sun round the shaded park:
two age-old friends,
(his walking stick, her umbrella),
sitting tight-lipped
on a green bench,

nodding away
at their quiet entourage of thoughts
(as the deer moved through the trees)
each holding a silent conversation
with the bowed head of the other.
Parks have always been like this —
trees, like dry litmus,
that burn a fetid red and leaves
falling like stunned butterflies

onto quiet people
who watch evenings draw in.
A long-legged spider
waves from a branch above
their hushed forms
casting off rainbow-dust
onto his still head,
her blue hat.
Together, they watch for him.
The fear of being locked in
makes them watch for the man
with the keys.

Eventually the web is broken.
The whistle blows.
The seagulls scream.
In quiet acquiescence they rise
taking each other's arm
through the streets of the town,
as the moon moves round the earth
and the earth moves round the moon,
his awkward walk, her prim feet,
going up the stairs,

having left nothing unspoken.

3. If It's Twilight

If it's twilight,
'the crack between the worlds',

can you imagine

an old man coming through the park,
butterflies singing round his head,
saying 'hey now', 'hey now' with his hands
as he shuffles along
jingling his keys?
All that is ordinary has kept him satisfied,
and all that is extraordinary is making him wary.
He comes out of his gate lodge
like a man out of a tale
told to children.
He is our summer companion from a dream,
someone who will disappear out of our lives.
He stands where everyone must leave —
at the point in the story
where you put down the book —
and then closes the gates on the flowers,
closes the gates on the glasshouses,
brings down the blinds on the birds
that are forever carrying the green of the trees
from tree to tree,

closes the gates,
pockets his watch.
Enough is enough.

Conditions

The gates are open

and in the meadow
a tall, stern man is making
smell-of-the-summer hay
with his wife,
and his brother's son.

The son's girlfriend
sells fine, dreamy dresses
in Mullingar, Westmeath,
and she has a little
money put by.

The son himself
will inherit the farm
from the flagons to the hollows,
the oak to the ash, when all
in the field are dead.

(His father
beat the tall man up
for some forgotten reason
when they were both
young men.)

The graceful wife
of the stern man
working, working
in the cloudless meadow
is childless

but there is nothing
under the sun,
no change she'd make,

she says, if she had her life
to live over again.

Though I'd like, said her husband,
to see it all done
and finished with
in a single day, if that
were possible.

And then it rains, it pours,
and crows alight with their young
on the bars when the gates are closed
by her, running half-heartedly
after the men in the rain.

As It Was

Sitting up with you
late into the night
means having
a good head

for heights.

❧

She cooks
breakfast in late
April, her hair in
a net. Our constant
arguments

are heated by love.

❧

Li Po
has circles
under his eyes
from the drink

like the dark
circles on stormy
nights

under the moon.

❧

Reilly's child,
the wild-eyed,
constantly carrying
a strange feather

through the granny's kitchen.

❧ ☙

In the allotment
an ordinary man,
his trousers covered in dirt,

puts the finishing
touches
to the rose

while the underground flies past.

❧ ☙

As we made love
each of your previous lovers
was present

and all of mine
strangely absent;
they had better things to do,

I suppose.

❧ ☙

If I follow the roots
of the ash out
I will come to water

silver-grey
for my lady's
shoe-buckles.

❧ ☙

I see you've finished
The Female Orgasm —
dare I ask

what you're reading now.

❧ ☙

The cat pushes out
her paws with a lazy purr
and begins peddling

round your breast.
Water, cold as winter,

bursts from the four brass taps.

Domestic Lives

for Dallan and Anne-Marie

1. The Circus

Signs of debris on the road this morning —
A wounded hedgehog and a dead young rabbit.
Admonished, we inspect these dreadful ruins and push
 the water back.
A thousand strings have been added to the lute.

Then do you remember the advancing clowns
And the horrendous roar of the elephants;
Or how you took that first drunken walk across the room,
Gathering breath, that you might have ample time for such
 adventures?

Long I looked into your eyes to see your life so far
From when you were nursed by fluorescent light, dressed
 in blood
And pushed down the forgotten corridor.

All cows now are elephants.
The fields for you are permanent circuses,
And we your bearded, petulant clowns.

2. *Veterans*

Oh we are both veterans of many household wars,
The sunny morning is laboured by your dry tears,
And yet you trace, carefully, the nose and eyes,
The sleeping face of your mother

With untrained, shy fingers, yet so assured
It shames the calculated passion of me, her lover.
You touch all parts of the body with the same polite discovery.
Your heroes are young men aged six or seven

On bikes or strolling or chasing their sisters of eleven.
Me, I fell in love with sixty-year-old men
But can never have that impartial love again.

When I speak for you or me we cannot hear what she is saying
And for you so far language is only a game.
You will discover my failures when, at last, you waken her
with words.

3. Perhaps You Are Too Human

Perhaps you are too human to bear these credentials
Of understatement, exaggeration I heap on you.
But it is not your innocence I would celebrate.
It is the willfulness, the amiable tyranny.

Because you cannot answer I am free
To sketch the tension and muscles in your hand,
To delight in how sexual and frightening you are,
In your laced boots, fair-face, milk-face.

I am no more your father than you are my son.
You have become the first real portrait of my life
And I can choose the profits and the forfeiture.

When you are my age you will sketch me so.
All men above sixty and children below two
Will not be denied you.

4. *If I Slap You*

If I slap you, how far will that resound,
Will it go deeper in you than me?
We would willingly suspend all screams
But you will not, neither of tears or laughter.

There is hardly one demonstrative truth
Or what will bear a repetition of the truth.
The pram fills up with cherry blossom.
The Queen's band parades down Sunday Street.

I cannot stand your barbarous tears.
I will hear them for years.
The sunny day

Is blackened out.
And of course I imagine your death
More often than my own.

5. I Dreamt, Said Heathcliff

I dreamt, said Heathcliff, I was sleeping
The last sleep by that sleeper, my heart stopped
And my cheek frozen against her. We are frozen here,
Too practical to think of love.

You climb the trees in the orchard
And lurk in the Christmas tree wood.
I am crushed underfoot in a drunken brawl
While the dancers weave in the old Town Hall.

To reach home
I have to break the ice
That has formed round everything:

The ice round the moon,
The ice round your breast,
The ice round mine.

6. Certainly, This Marriage

Certainly, this marriage is not the crucial place
To organise your life. It sustains cruel gods
And self-perpetuating societies. It is never really over
And is sometimes the cul-de-sac of love.

Nevertheless, here we are as we'll never be again.
You will for some years endure our entrepreneurship,
And fear, jaded child, the moth under the blanket
Or the crust of bread that found its way to your feet

As you will distrust the tempers of parenthood.
All our arguments to preserve your faith
Mean nothing. You will be forever alone

Notwithstanding the evidences of art and laughter.
But today the crushed rose-and-white chestnut blooms fill
the path;
Tomorrow your small nails will attack the untuned guitar.

My Kiss Too

Perhaps the son is saying,

'I see shadows,
I see the shape of something
I was supposed to believe in
And I thought

Cities is the life,
A dead trout in a stream
Is only a slack breast
On some street corner.'

And perhaps the son is dreaming,
'I'll not live the dreary fear
When I grow up.
I will not repeat myself.

I will not say silver when I mean lead.
I will not say poor when I mean power.
Let the door of the house of your heart break down
To my incessant thundering.'

So first, I found endless things,
A kiss for the child on the edge of sleep,
A kiss and then, waiting on an image of us,
I want the child's wants, my kiss too.

London 1975

O Woman

O woman for whom
I have withdrawn

From naming the brilliant things of the earth
Less they might lose their vividness,

Can we now without myth
Sustain the emptiness?

Silence has invaded the house.
The water does not move.

These are the two guilty quiets of all:
A boat at the door, our sealed lips.

I cannot hear the wild duck.
There is only one swan.

The silence of the waters
Goes on and on.

PART TWO
DOONEEL
1989-1992

After the Silence

The moon stood
Like a drunk
Looking up the street
Wondering,

Is this the street,
Is this the town,
What happened,
And who did I meet?

Oh there were happier times,
There's no denying the fact,
But they're over.
It's done. That's that.

The New Town

The first days I went to town
I used to pass them;
In time found out they were
The hospital, the asylum.

From the beginning I had
An affinity for both.
The General I walked to from Glencar,
St Columba's from The Point.

In one my hand was put in plaster,
In the other I was given librium.
A couple of years I spent
Cocooned in delerium,

Till language like a nurse
Pitched her tent without a sound.
Enough light here to write by,
Enough remorse to put it down.

But my mind didn't flower.
The break refused to set.
My hand will never make a fist,
And you haunt me yet.

Harebell

for Leland

1

Harebell!
Clock of the tides,
Woman in a bonnet,
Wearer of two blues,

Send word to the orange-tree
And do not keep your head averted
As you often do
When you send word.

I am thinking
Of making a journey
Out into the world again.
What is happening where I've never been?

2

Harebell! Stem in the glass with lowered eyes,
Don't deny me with that continual shake of the head —
Just nod in my direction. Harebell!
Cup a keen ear to the sea!

Any news of the orange-tree?
Harebell! Flute of the ocean! Flutterer!
Tell me all I need to know.
Has someone died on the Mediterranean?

Is the orange-tree as I imagine it?
Nettle-green with a wide skirt over a wide space
And underneath a plaza swept clean
For fruit to fall?

Do Spaniards sit under its thatch?
Can I drink wine there and keep my head?
Harebell! Friend! My blue, tall confessor
Of a woman, look at your beautiful foot!

3

One head, one foot, one root.
Are you the lady that was here last year?
Are you another, then another,
Mother and husband to yourself?

Are you the one that was in Ballyliffin?
Do you come back as yourself each time
Or have I fallen in love with a succession of women,
Head averted, each different, just dressed the same?

4

Harebell! I am frightened of your simplicity.
Are you saying yes or are you saying no?
Harebell! Your silence will drown the seashell
While I am far from home.

This year again, a hint of blue will turn into you.
Hooded monk, you are up before everyone!
With your delicate cup and your delicate waist
Stay with me as far as the orange-tree.

The Five Senses

The steady hiss of the tilly,
The groaning rain barrel;

Boiled bollan,
Baled hay;

The fossil on the stone
Where the soap sits;

Tall moon-white daisies
On the bank, shaking,

And sea salt
In the sea mist.

The Hares on Oyster Island

for Inor

Praise be the hares on Oyster
As they curl on the stone beach
And look across at Rosses!

Do they take that shape to look good —
A soul looking toward heaven
But not ready to go yet?

When I take the binoculars and see the blur of the hare
Separating itself from the blur of the stones
The disturbance eases.

The hare that always turns back a moment
To look steadfastly into the sights
Of the rifle that will kill him

Bounces forward, looks back into my eyes,
Bounces forward, looks into my daughter's eyes,
And settles comfortable,

Comforting me in my turn.
Praise be the hares on Oyster Island!
Put there by huntsmen. Loved by poets.

And gone at last beyond the reach of dogs.
They eat with the sheep and the guinea hens,
And run short distances between bouts of contemplation.

May they have long lives,
The hares that afford us a break
From the language that would explain them.

May they be shot straight through the heart
By a woman in a boat, and then wake to hear
The bells of the halyards.

That nature allow me
A moment to look back the way I've come
And feel, this time, I'm safe for a while.

If we sit a while longer before we move on
That the scream never come!
That I finish what I've begun.

To be like the hares that sit out there beyond smell,
Beyond touch, secure on their pads as they sit
Up and remember!

May the hares increase! The inspiration
They give me prosper. That I learn to make of isolation
And fear a grand thing.

Let the hare sit! Let the hare sit on the moon!
And may we be all shot straight through the heart
By a woman in a boat.

Grounded at Annie-Come-Ashore

The sea is on nights.
The horizon is an empty factory floor.
If you step outside
You'll see the day shift

Pass the night shift
On the second shore.
The lights from the airport
Stream across the bed of the ocean

But someone has missed
The bend for home.
They kept going
Till they could go

No longer. Stand at Annie-Come-Ashore
You'll see the ship grounded
Like a casino at Ballincar,
Love, with all its lights on.

And in the third house from the left
I'm stuck high and dry
In a fiction that won't end
And a love affair that ended.

Like the stranded Poles I'm waiting
For the high waters of late September
To make me buoyant again,
To fill each side of me,

Till then I'm here
Unable to carry on.
Mark me on the second beach
Waiting for the pilot

Or on the prom at night
Watching the silent gulls in a gale.
Hundreds, falling in one behind the other,
Just above the water, for hours,

Steadfastly.

Rosses Point

As many have walked this beach
As sat on Thomas Hardy's seat,

And if they were counted maybe many more.
A doctor from London, a priest from Ecuador;

Yeats himself who was ten foot tall
To see all he saw,

Sydney Bernard, in the late afternoon,
Just out from the word-processor in his room.

We'd pass without a word
Nursing a hurt,

In the horrors of sobriety,
The discontent of solitude.

Austie himself who spent his life on ship
Travels the sands on his new hip.

A dead ass which came in in a storm
Is buried three times and is three times reborn.

What would the living do
If they had not the dead to see to?

Mountbatten, Jack B., Norwegian sailors.
Annie-Come-Ashore, the Bruens, Sligo jailors.

Each walks to the edge of the surf.
One life for them was not enough.

Towards evening come nurses from Cregg,
On the first beach a Christian mission is fed.

Sometimes a golfer will stand on a sand dune,
A bishop appears, or two nuns, or no one.

The dead have a certain momentum.
Sometimes it's hard to keep up with them.

I fall into step with some other
Who came up for the day with his mother

In a different century,
A sprightly lad, malevolent, pernickety.

The three beaches are crowded though you can't see a soul.
The practical, the comfortable, the vulnerable.

And what do they see as they turn to come back?
The living out swimming, or the solitude they lack?

How will I be when I have not the second or the third
To walk on at night looking for the right word?

There are Nights

There are nights that the sea smells of cows,
Of warm bedding they've lain in,
Their dung and straw

And steaming breath,
The hay they've eaten,
The way they nurse their calves.

You can hear by the pier
The slow plod of their hooves,
The floundering of their swelling rumps,

And a sweetness comes in off the sea
As if milking had just finished.
Pails are emptied on Coney,

Halyards ring on the moored yachts,
Someone lets go a rope,
And the oxen move on

Slowly towards Mayo.

Two Moons

The moon above Sligo
Is not
The moon above Mayo.

On Looking Up at the Night Sky above Lough Conn

You put a book down
And go out under the stars
And stand aghast
At how much

You miss
Behind the closed door,
How much goes on
When you're not there.

Stars
That have gone back
Into history
Are shining like new towns

For the traveller;
They tell us where home is
And what will happen us
In the hereafter.

Each pulse of unerring light
Marks a place on the map
Of our ignorance
And wisdom.

And each time I look away
The darkness comes with me
And the lived-in stars.
Then it happens.

I find myself
Weightless, up there
Looking down
On myself,

Standing alone
By the birdless waters
Of Lough Conn. Behind me
A door is open,

A dog is circling,
A radio playing.
I have been looking up for as long
As I can at the heavens.

I step back
A bit from the dark waters.
Soon the door closes.
The dog whines.

The Next Room

When I heard
A cough from the next room
I thought it was Maisie
Who has long cleared ninety
Clearing phlegm

But the next room is an unoccupied room
Of a fisherman's holiday home
On the banks of Lough Conn.
There's no one here
But myself.

The cough could have been caused
By anything. By a water-pipe. By some sound
Buried in the house.
And yet it's Maisie's cough
As much as anything.

Maisie coughing on an Afton in *The Magnet*,
Maisie coughing on an Afton in the Town Hall,
On the three steps below the altar,
Along the corridor,
In the yard,

Maisie coughing in her old room above Main Street
Where she used to sit looking into three mirrors
With the radio on loud. Surrounded by powder balls,
Perfumes with long stems.
Talc. Mass cards.

The three of her coughing, polite and assured.
Or there's her present non-smoker's cough in
 the bungalow
In Cootehill that follows or precedes

A bout of being sick,
That is girlish

And sad, and followed
By intense sentences of grief.
The cough I hear could be any of these:
The business woman walking up the entry;
The blind lady in front of the TV;

The girl who never stood by Lough Conn.
And yet she is as surely in the next room with
 the cataracts removed
As she is anywhere. We take the next room
With us everywhere, the unoccupied room
Where they all live

Whom we have met,
Who lived out part of their lives
A little way along the stairs from us,
Who lived above us
Or below.

Next door they prepare for sleep
Or wake wondering where they are.
We're still here, says Maisie, sitting assured
 before the three of her,
With the radio on in a room she has never been in,
Coughing absentmindedly. Thinking.

Neighbours' Lights

On fine blue nights
My neighbours farm
The sky.

On the Bent
The Currids and the Carroways
Are behind the Plough.

Towards Raghley
The Pole Star lights up
Men in a field of just-turned hay.

There's a new star
Rocking in the coal boat of the Poles
Beyond Inishmurray,

Sligo, a sorrowing drunk,
Makes its way home
Along the swill of the Milky Way.

Killybegs and Ballyshannon
Are villages open late
In the heavens,

And driving towards Easkey
A fisherman's car
Is a shooting star.

They've set Pleiades
In the field
Next to my field,

But besides Venus
Who sits after ten
In Jimmy Foley's kitchen

Our nearest neighbour
Is the list of the moon
In the sea

Drawing its scythe
With a clean sweep of light
Through a black scraw of cloud

At low water.

On High Street

He emerges onto the street
And stops as if lost,
Then pretends to carry on.
For a while there he was
Back among the harmful reveries of the psyche
To see what was still standing.
His thoughts are familiar
But someone else is thinking them now,
Saying, this is enough, this will do.

This will do for now.
The things he saw today
Near Boyle. The starlings I saw
The other evening over Jimmy Foley's.
Like me he is hoarding
These pleasures and shocked
By how little they matter
When the blackness falls,
When the knife is thrust into the bowel.

He stands on High Street
With each man he sees
Remote as Virgil or Homer.
The path he planned
For the day has left him.
Where he was going
Has ceased to exist.
His shined shoes grow heavier.
He half-raises his hand

To a local woman
He thought he knew.
The black bag of laundry
He's carrying
Fills out like a balloon.

Some time ago
All disturbances were removed
And yet inexplicably,
Here they are again.

And he knows it.
I can see he knows it.
Standing there
On High Street on a Tuesday afternoon
He scans the pavement opposite
And his eyes light on mine.
Immediately he turns and goes
Wherever he was going.
And I, same as he, continue on.

Prayer

'To pray is to wish another well.'
— Frances Molloy

Sometimes I am bewildered
By all this foolish energy
Battering away
Miles from people.

I envy those
Who live upriver
At the quiet source.
Here we are forever

Stepping between
The incoming roar
Of life and the tides
That carry death out.

They are right
Who had long ago
The sense to collect
In great numbers

In sea-cities
To protect themselves.
Men should put miles
Between themselves

And the sea
From which they spring.
You should not stay too long
In your mother's house.

Mourn her
From some place inland.
Praise her
To a new woman

Raised in the midlands
Whose birds and trees
Keep autumn and spring.
What wakes us here at night

Is not something
We've imagined.
It's the real thing.
The parent ocean

Giving birth,
And the sound of all who ever existed
Surfacing and striking
For shore

Into the dreams
Of sea-folk in their beds.
The first tractor rises
On the stones of a path,

And smoke rears
From a chimney.
Winds harry the cliffs.
This is the new day.

I search the words for it
And would break out
Into prayer,
If I could.

Or if I knew
One prayer to the sea
I'd say it. Instead
I remember

Your definition
Of prayer —
To wish another well.
This is all we can do.

Rain is Coming

for Seán and Sheila

The swifts
Skim low over the stones,
Turn out over the sea,
Swing up over the cliffs
And round the house
And round the house,

Flat, narrow,
Beautiful,
Quick as an arrow
The birds of Loughaun
Say 'Rain is coming,'
'Rain is coming,'

'Your home is a shell,'
'Your body is a shell,'
Low and fast
About the gable,
Small and dark-eyed,
Nimble-shouldered,

They fly
Into a black gale,
Chase each other
Through sea-light,
Dart past me
In the chair

Where I sit
Amazed by birds
That never land
But make love

Somewhere up there
Beyond our heads

And fall asleep after
And fall and fall
On currents of air
Till they wake
Just before they strike
The earth,

The shapeless sea.
They brake
For a split second
To think which way now.
Wings folded back,
They dash

At an angle
Towards a point
Of turbulence
Which for them
Means joy.
Winds that

Drive men crazy
Are ecstasy for birds
That have just awoken
From making love,
That have been falling
All night

To earth.
Good for the soul
To watch swifts in September,
Seated on a chair

By the gable
As they fly

The silent patterns
Of love,
Flying low
And close,
Dangerously close
To each other,

Round the house,
Round the house,
Rain is coming,
Rain is coming,
Your house is a shell,
Your body is a shell,

Round the house,
Round the house,
Over the sea,
Up the cliffs,
Over the roof,
Rain is coming,

Rain is coming!

The Roads

Oh the road to Belmullet —
You'll not be on it,
My love and my darling.

Oh the road to Clonmany —
The green finch
Is all that there is.

Winter Nights

for Jimmy Foley

On winter nights
Myself and Jimmy Foley
Climb out of bed
And put on our wings.

Jimmy's for Ellen's;
I'm for the Horseshoe.
So we compromise
And settle for Carney.

Everybody there knows Jimmy.
They all come up
To admire the way
He is himself

And yet never
Leaves another out,
Not even me,
For when I want to go

He's with me.
We have to fly to a funeral,
We have to see friends of his
In Maugheroy.

There's shopping to be done,
Fish gutted and salted,
People to talk to in Wine Street,
Women to see on Harmony Hill.

And then it's back
Through the clean cold air

Till we hit the mists.
In the mists we lose touch.

Well, we have an arrangement.
He goes to his house
And I go to mine,
And whichever of us

Has his light lit first
Can expect the other to tea.
Always it's Jimmy's lamp
Lights up,

And although I'm often
Tired enough
To want to sleep
And stay where I am

Next to the few things
I know best
By the time I fly to Jimmy's
I'm a new man.

We leave our wings
To the left of the fire
To dry out
And smoke Woodbines.

These are our winter nights —
Flying over Maugheroy,
Then sitting by the fire
Waiting on our wings to dry.

The Ballyconnell Colours

for Helen

In the late afternoon
When the light is failing
The new window in the door
Turns the house into a desolate shop
That looks out on a windy parish
As I sit within
With nothing to tell
By the table.

The worst hours
Are those between three and seven,
Too early to light the candles,
Too late for the sun
To reach in. I sit
Waiting — no one comes —
Waiting for the real comforting dark
To fall.

Around eight
The shop closes. You come home.
Night falls like a shutter.
Everything is put away
Till morning, and the sea,
Blowing west,
Is sheer white.
The house

Turns into a ship
And rides out to sea.
We listen to forecasts
From Malin — west-south-west,
Forty-five miles an hour.
Rising rapidly.

Thunder strikes
The earth under the bed.

We are sheltering
In Donlons' boat.
The road to the house
Grows taut
As a mooring line
That attaches us
To the far mainland.
The house stays firm.

It's we who break free
In the storm
And are brought out
Across the bumping sea
Beyond the bar
To a dangerous swell
Of dangerous lights.
And at the moment of peril

When we might be lost
Forever comes the gentle
Tug of wakening.
The wind still there, or not there.
Where have we been?
I do not know —
Each night further out,
Beyond dreaming even,

To find next morning
The beach is facing another way
And the ship we travelled
Safely in has turned
Into a studio.

The storm has painted
The stones battleship grey,
The eaves canary yellow,

The door
Peacock blue.
These are the sea colours
Of Ballyconnell.
And the north-west gable is
A wind-toughened sail
Resting before
The next storm.

You go down the road
We cast off nightly in our dreams,
And Jack Donlon comes
Across the fields. The bare shop
Has opened again. There's a new give
In the earth. The McSweeneys
Gather. We talk of
Murders, suicides,

And fairies.
That's what we talk of
Here in Dooneel.
And when all the folk
Are gone I wait for the darkness
Impatiently again,
Through the mindless
Hallucinatory hours

Of the afternoon,
Trying to find
Space for it all —
Yourself, the silence of gales,

The unyielding stars,
And the white seal pup on the rocks
Thrown up here,
Like myself,

In a storm.

Acknowledgements

Acknowledgements are due to the editors and publishers of *Cyphers*, *The Drumlin*, *Force 10 in Mayo*, *Icarus*, *The Inward Eye*, *Jaguar* (Collins Harvill) and *Soundings* in which some of these poems were published first.

The author wishes to thank Seán Golden in Barcelona where most of this collection was put together in November 1991.